PHILIPPINES
TRAVEL GUIDE 2024;
EXPLORING THE BEST OF PHILIPPINES ON LOW BUDGET.

BEN CARTER

Reserved rights. Without the publisher's prior written consent, no part of this book may be duplicated, copied, or communicated in any way, including by photocopying, recording, or other electronic or mechanical techniques, unless expressly authorized by copyright laws.

Contents

Chapter One: INTRODUCTION 12

    Brief Overview of the Country: 13

        Geography: 13

        Culture: 14

        History: 15

        Language: 15

        Cuisine: 15

        Biodiversity: 16

        Contemporary Life: 16

Chapter Two: Getting Started 18

    Planning Your Trip 19

        Best Times to Visit 20

        Budgeting Tips 20

        Cultural Sensitivity 21

    Visa and Entry Requirements 22

        Visa Information 22

        Entry Regulations 23

        Extended Stays and Permits 23

        Travel Insurance 23

    Currency and Money Matters 24

        Philippine Peso (PHP) 24

Banking and ATMs	25
Budgeting Strategies	25
Currency Exchange Tips	25
Language and Communication	26
Official Languages	26
Language Diversity	26
Basic Communication Tips	27
Translation Apps and Resources	27
Chapter Three: Essential Travel Information	**28**
Weather and Climate	29
Overview of the Climate	29
Tag-init (Hot Dry Season)	30
Tag-ulan (Rainy Season)	30
Tag-lamig (Cool Dry Season)	31
Typhoon Season	31
Packing Tips	32
Health and Safety Tips	33
Health Precautions	33
Medical Facilities	34
Safety Tips	35
Local Customs and Etiquette	36
Greetings and Politeness	37
Clothing Etiquette	37

Social Customs 38
Dining Etiquette 38

Chapter Four: Regions and Islands 40

Luzon 40
Historical Landmarks 41
Banaue Rice Terraces 44
Visayas 48

Chapter Five: Top Attractions 57

Palawan 57
Puerto Princesa Underground River 57
El Nido's Stunning Islands 59
Sunset at Corong-Corong 61
Bohol 62
Chocolate Hills 62
Tarsier Conservation Area 64

Chapter Six: Activities and Adventures 67

Scuba Diving in Tubbataha Reefs Natural Park 67
Hiking in Mount Pulag 71
Island Hopping in Coron 74

Chapter Seven: Culinary Delights 78

Filipino Cuisine Overview 78
Flavorful Fusion 78
Signature Dishes 79

Street Food Extravaganza 80
    Sweet Indulgences 81
    Regional Specialties..................................... 81
Must-Try Dishes... 82
    Sinigang 82
    Lechon Kawali... 83
    Chicken Adobo 83
    Kare-Kare.. 83
    Halo-Halo 84
Street Food Adventures 84
    Isaw 84
    Fish Balls... 85
    Balut 85
    Taho.. 85
    Turon 86

Chapter Eight: Cultural Experiences............................ 87

Festivals and Celebrations.................................. 87
    Sinulog Festival... 87
    Ati-Atihan Festival 87
    Panagbenga Festival.................................... 88
    Pahiyas Festival 88
    Dinagyang Festival....................................... 89
    Moriones Festival... 89

- Kadayawan Festival 90
- MassKara Festival 90

Traditional Arts and Crafts 91
- Weaving in Ifugao 91
- Pottery in Sagada 92
- T'nalak Weaving in South Cotabato 92
- Shellcraft in Cebu 93

Historical Sites and Museums 94
- Intramuros in Manila 94
- Banaue Rice Terraces 94
- National Museum of the Philippines 95
- Corregidor Island 95

Chapter Nine: Practical Tips 97

Transportation within the Philippines 97
- Domestic Flights 97
- Buses and Vans 98
- Jeepneys and Tricycles 99
- Ferries and Boats 99
- Renting Vehicles 100
- Transportation Apps 100
- Traveling Off-Peak 101

Accommodations 102
- Diverse Options 102

Communication and Connectivity 103
    SIM Cards 103
    Wi-Fi Availability.. 104
Packing Tips... 104
    Weather-Appropriate Clothing................................... 105
    Travel Adapters.. 105
    Essentials................................. 106
    Daypack 107
    Money Matters... 107
    Light Snacks................................. 108

Chapter Ten: Sustainability and Responsible Travel............ 109
Ecotourism Initiatives...................................... 109
    Tubbataha Reefs Natural Park...................................... 109
    Masungi Georeserve 110
    Apo Reef Natural Park.. 111
    Mayon Skyline View Deck 111
    Banaue Rice Terraces 112
    Responsible Island Hopping in Palawan...................... 113
    Environmental Awareness in Sagada 113
Responsible Diving and Snorkeling Practices 115
    Coral Conservation....................................... 115
    Sustainable Diving Operators 116
    Marine Life Etiquette................................... 117

Supporting Local Communities 118
    Local Businesses 118
    Cultural Respect 119
    Community-based Tourism 119
    Volunteer Opportunities 120

Conclusion 122

Final Thoughts 122
Memories to Take Home 123

What to see & do in Philippines

Philippines
WORLD'S MOST ICONIC TROPICAL DESTINATIONS

The choice of things to do in the Philippines is very impressive, thanks to the country's incredible variety of landscapes.

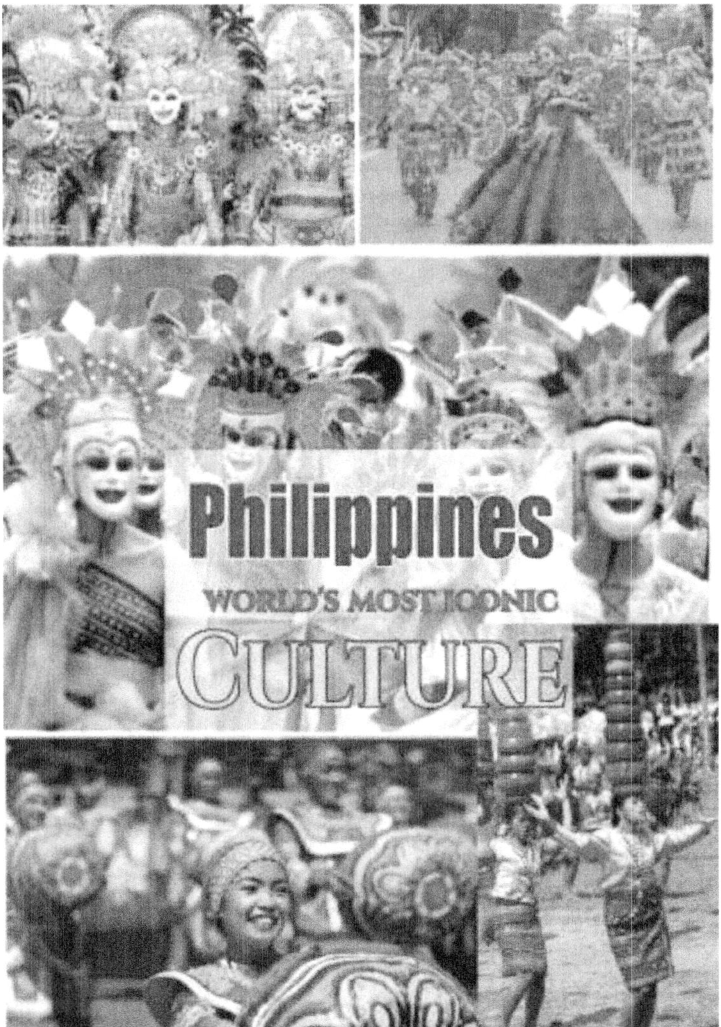
Philippines
WORLD'S MOST ICONIC
CULTURE

Chapter One:
Introduction

Welcome to the Philippines, an archipelago of over 7,000 islands scattered across the western Pacific Ocean. Renowned for its natural beauty, vibrant culture, and warm hospitality, the Philippines is a destination that has something to offer everyone.

The Philippines, an archipelago in Southeast Asia, welcomes you with open arms to a land of vibrant culture, stunning landscapes, and warm hospitality. As you step onto its shores, you're about to embark on a journey that promises a rich tapestry of experiences, from bustling metropolises to serene tropical islands.

Brief Overview of the Country

Geography:

The Philippines is an archipelago consisting of 7,641 islands, each offering a unique blend of natural wonders. From the white-sand beaches of Boracay to the lush rice terraces of Banaue and the diverse marine life in Palawan, the country's geography is a testament to its breathtaking beauty.

Culture:

Diverse and deeply rooted, Filipino culture is a fusion of indigenous traditions, Spanish influence from centuries of colonization, and modern global dynamics. The warmth and friendliness of the Filipino people, known for their genuine smiles and hospitable nature, create an atmosphere of immediate belonging.

History:

With a history that spans pre-colonial times through Spanish rule to American occupation, the Philippines has a storied past. Historical sites like Intramuros in Manila stand as tangible reminders of this rich heritage, inviting travelers to step back in time and explore the nation's narrative.

Language:

Filipino, based on Tagalog, is the official language, but English is widely spoken, making communication with locals relatively easy for international visitors. This linguistic diversity reflects the country's openness to the world.

Cuisine:

A gastronomic adventure awaits in the Philippines, where local delicacies such as adobo, sinigang, and lechon showcase a blend of flavors. Street food stalls to fine-dining restaurants offer a diverse culinary landscape that tantalizes taste buds and adds a flavorful dimension to your journey.

Biodiversity:

The Philippines boasts incredible biodiversity, both on land and underwater. From the tarsiers in Bohol to the vibrant coral reefs in Tubbataha Reefs Natural Park, nature lovers will find themselves immersed in a haven of unique flora and fauna.

Contemporary Life:

While the Philippines embraces its cultural roots, it also thrives in the contemporary world. Dynamic cities like Manila and Cebu buzz with activity, offering modern amenities, shopping districts, and a lively nightlife, creating a harmonious blend of tradition and progress.

CHAPTER TWO: GETTING STARTED

Embarking on your journey to the Philippines requires thoughtful preparation to ensure a smooth and enriching travel experience. Start by meticulously planning your itinerary, considering the diverse offerings of this archipelagic paradise. Understand the best times to visit, budget effectively, and embrace cultural sensitivity to fully immerse yourself in the way of life.

Planning Your Trip

Embark on the first steps of your Philippine adventure by carefully planning your trip. Whether you seek the bustling energy of city life or the tranquility of island escapes, crafting a well-thought-out itinerary ensures you make the most of your time in this diverse archipelago.

Best Times to Visit

Navigate the nuances of Philippine weather patterns and discover the optimal times to visit various regions. Uncover the ideal seasons for beach vacations, mountain treks, and cultural festivals to tailor your journey to your preferences.

Budgeting Tips

Gain insights into managing your travel expenses effectively. From accommodation options to transportation choices, understanding the local cost of living allows you to plan a trip that aligns with your budget while still experiencing the best the Philippines has to offer.

Cultural Sensitivity

Immerse yourself in Filipino culture by familiarizing yourself with local customs and traditions. Learn about appropriate attire, greeting customs, and other cultural nuances to ensure a respectful and enriching travel experience.

Visa and Entry Requirements

Visa Information

Navigate the visa requirements for entering the Philippines. Whether you're eligible for visa-free entry or need to secure a visa in advance, understanding the necessary documentation is crucial for a smooth arrival and stay.

Entry Regulations

Explore the specifics of entry regulations, including customs and immigration procedures. From required vaccinations to customs declarations, equip yourself with the knowledge needed to breeze through arrival processes and start your Philippine adventure hassle-free.

Extended Stays and Permits

For travelers planning longer stays or engaging in specific activities, such as volunteering or business ventures, delve into the details of extended stay options and necessary permits. Ensure you comply with local regulations to make the most of your time in the Philippines.

Travel Insurance

Prioritize your well-being by considering travel insurance options. Learn about coverage for medical emergencies, trip cancellations, and other unforeseen events to travel with peace of mind and confidence.

Currency and Money Matters

Philippine Peso (PHP)

`Familiarize yourself with the official currency of the Philippines, the Philippine Peso (PHP). Explore currency denominations, exchange rates, and tips for handling money, ensuring a seamless financial experience throughout your journey.

Banking and ATMs

Navigate the Philippine banking system and discover the convenience of ATMs for accessing cash. Learn about widely accepted credit cards, banking hours, and reliable methods for managing your finances while traveling.

Budgeting Strategies

Craft a practical budget for your Philippine adventure. Gain insights into average costs for accommodation, meals, transportation, and activities to optimize your spending and make the most of your travel funds.

Currency Exchange Tips

Maximize the value of your money by understanding the best practices for currency exchange. Explore reputable exchange services, be aware of potential fees, and stay informed about favorable exchange rates during your stay.

Language and Communication

Official Languages

Dive into the linguistic tapestry of the Philippines, a nation with two official languages—Filipino and English. Learn about the prevalence of English in daily communication and discover key Filipino phrases to enhance your travel experience.

Language Diversity

Explore the linguistic diversity across regions and islands. Uncover local dialects and languages spoken in specific areas, adding a layer of cultural richness to your interactions with the warm and welcoming Filipino people.

Basic Communication Tips

Arm yourself with essential communication tips to navigate daily interactions. From greetings and expressions of gratitude to understanding common phrases, enhance your ability to connect with locals and immerse yourself in the vibrant Filipino culture.

Translation Apps and Resources

Consider utilizing translation apps and resources to bridge language gaps. Discover user-friendly tools that can enhance your communication, making your travel experience more enjoyable and ensuring smooth interactions with locals.

Chapter Three: Essential Travel Information

For a peacefully travel you have to consider the below information.

Weather and Climate

Overview of the Climate

The Philippines boasts a tropical maritime climate, making it an ideal destination for sun-seekers and nature enthusiasts. The archipelago experiences three distinct seasons: Tag-init (hot dry), Tag-ulan (rainy), and Tag-lamig (cool dry), each contributing to the country's diverse and vibrant landscapes.

Tag-init (Hot Dry Season)

Duration: March to May

The hot dry season brings warm temperatures and clear skies, making it a popular time for beach vacations and outdoor activities. Temperatures can soar, particularly in lowland areas, so it's advisable to stay hydrated and use sun protection. This season is ideal for exploring the pristine beaches of Palawan, Boracay, and other island paradises.

Tag-ulan (Rainy Season)

Duration: June to November

The rainy season is characterized by frequent rain showers and typhoons. While rain can be intense, especially in August and September, it often comes in short bursts, leaving room for exploration between showers. The lush landscapes come alive during this season, and it's an excellent time for nature lovers to witness the vibrant greenery of rice terraces and rainforests.

Tag-lamig (Cool Dry Season)

Duration: December to February

The cool dry season brings milder temperatures and cooler evenings, making it a pleasant time to explore various regions of the Philippines. This season is popular for cultural festivals, such as the Ati-Atihan in Kalibo and the Panagbenga Festival in Baguio. It's also an ideal time for hiking adventures, particularly in the mountainous areas of Luzon and Mindanao.

Typhoon Season

Caution: The Philippines is prone to typhoons, especially during the rainy season. Travelers should stay informed about weather updates, particularly if visiting coastal or typhoon-prone areas. It's advisable to check weather forecasts regularly and follow local authorities' advice in case of severe weather warnings.

P‌ackin‌g Tips

Regardless of the season, packing essentials include lightweight clothing, swimwear, comfortable footwear for exploring, and rain gear during the rainy season. Sunscreen, insect repellent, and a reusable water bottle are must-haves for any traveler, ensuring a comfortable and enjoyable experience throughout diverse weather conditions.

Health and Safety Tips

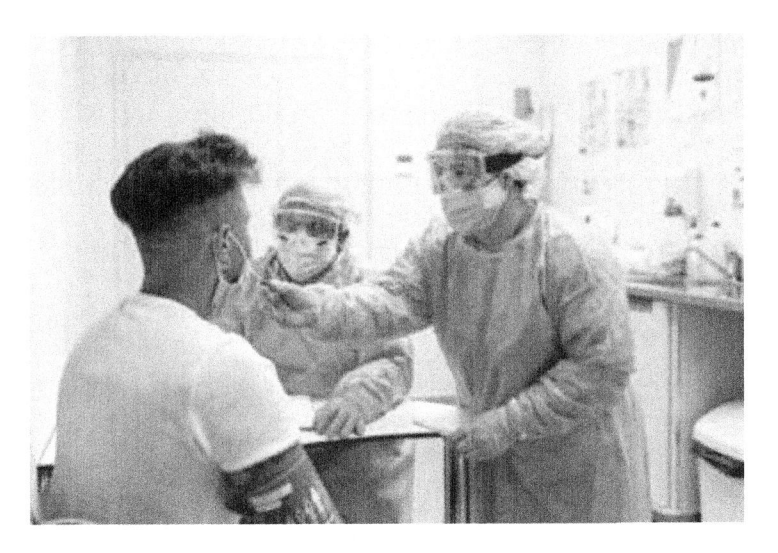

Health Precautions

Vaccinations: Before traveling to the Philippines, ensure that routine vaccinations are up-to-date. Depending on your travel plans, additional vaccines such as Hepatitis A and B, typhoid, and Japanese encephalitis may be recommended.

Water and Food Safety: Drink bottled or purified water and avoid consuming raw or undercooked food. Opt for freshly prepared meals from reputable establishments to minimize the risk of foodborne illnesses.

Mosquito-Borne Diseases: The Philippines is in a region where mosquito-borne diseases like dengue fever are prevalent. Use insect repellent, wear long sleeves and pants, and stay in accommodations with screened windows to minimize the risk of mosquito bites.

Medical Facilities

Health Insurance: Ensure you have comprehensive travel insurance that covers medical expenses. Confirm whether your insurance includes medical evacuation in case of emergencies.

Local Healthcare: Familiarize yourself with the locations of medical facilities and pharmacies in the areas you plan to visit. In major cities, you'll find well-equipped hospitals, but more remote areas may have limited medical services.

Medication and First Aid Kit: Carry a basic first aid kit with essential medications, including any prescribed medications, pain relievers, and remedies for common travel ailments.

Safety Tips

Transportation Safety: Choose reputable transportation options and prioritize safety over cost. Follow local traffic rules, use seatbelts, and exercise caution, especially when using public transportation.

Emergency Contacts: Save local emergency numbers and the contact information of your country's embassy or consulate. Share your itinerary with a trusted friend or family member.

Natural Hazards: Be aware of natural hazards such as typhoons and earthquakes. Stay informed about weather conditions and follow local authorities' advice during adverse weather events.

Local Customs and Etiquette

Greetings and Politeness

"Po" and "Opo": Use these words to show respect when responding to elders. "Po" is added to sentences, and "Opo" is a polite way of saying "yes."

Mano Po: A traditional gesture of respect, particularly towards elders, involves taking the hand of an elder and placing it on one's forehead.

Clothing Etiquette

Modesty: Dress modestly, especially when visiting religious sites. Avoid revealing clothing in conservative areas to show respect for local customs.

Removing Shoes: In Filipino homes, it's customary to remove shoes before entering. Follow the lead of your host or hostess.

Social Customs

Bayanihan: Embrace the Filipino spirit of community and cooperation. "Bayanihan" refers to the practice of neighbors helping each other, and you may encounter this sense of camaraderie during local events or festivals.

Respect for Elders: Filipinos hold great respect for elders. Listen attentively when elders speak, and avoid addressing them by their first names unless given permission.

Dining Etiquette

Utensil Use: Filipinos often use a fork and spoon rather than a knife and fork. It's customary to eat with the fork in the left hand and the spoon in the right.

Sharing Food: Filipino meals are often served "family-style," with everyone sharing from common dishes. It's polite to wait for the host to start before digging in.

Chapter Four: Regions and Islands

Luzon

Manila: Capital and Beyond

Gateway to the Philippines: Manila, the bustling capital, serves as the gateway to the Philippines, offering a vibrant blend of history, culture, and modernity. Nestled along the shores of Manila

Bay, this dynamic metropolis is a captivating introduction to the country's diversity.

Historical Landmarks

Intramuros: Step back in time within the walls of Intramuros, a historic district dating back to Spanish colonial times. Explore Fort Santiago, a citadel that played a significant role in Philippine history, and visit San Agustin Church, a UNESCO World Heritage Site.

Rizal Park: Pay homage to national hero Dr. Jose Rizal at Rizal Park, a sprawling green oasis in the heart of Manila. The park features monuments, gardens, and the Rizal Monument, an iconic symbol of Philippine independence.

Cultural Experiences

National Museum Complex: Immerse yourself in Filipino art, history, and culture at the National Museum Complex. Explore the National Museum of Fine Arts, the National Museum of Anthropology, and the National Museum of Natural History.

Cultural Shows and Performances: Experience the richness of Filipino culture through traditional performances. Witness vibrant folk dances, music, and theatrical productions that showcase the country's diverse heritage.

Modern Manila

Makati and Bonifacio Global City (BGC): Indulge in the modern side of Manila by exploring the business districts of Makati and BGC. Discover upscale shopping, dining, and entertainment options, as well as the impressive skyline that defines the city's contemporary charm.

Culinary Delights: Manila is a food lover's paradise, offering a wide array of culinary delights. From street food to high-end restaurants, savor Filipino specialties such as adobo, sinigang, and lechon.

Beyond Manila

Tagaytay: Embark on a short journey south of Manila to Tagaytay, known for its stunning views of Taal Volcano. Enjoy cool weather, visit the Picnic Grove, and indulge in local delicacies overlooking the picturesque Taal Lake.

Pampanga: Head north to Pampanga, the culinary capital of the Philippines. Explore heritage sites, indulge in Kapampangan cuisine, and experience the vibrant local culture.

Banaue Rice Terraces

Majestic Landscape

Architectural Marvel: The Banaue Rice Terraces, often referred to as the "Eighth Wonder of the World," stand as a testament to the ingenuity of the Ifugao people. Carved into the Cordillera

Mountains more than 2,000 years ago, these terraces showcase an ancient agricultural engineering marvel.

Cultural Heritage

Ifugao Heritage: Explore the cultural richness of the Ifugao people, who meticulously crafted the terraces using hand tools. Learn about their sustainable farming practices, passed down through generations, and the cultural significance of the terraces in Ifugao society.

Batad Rice Terraces: Venture beyond Banaue to the nearby village of Batad, home to the jaw-dropping amphitheater-shaped rice terraces. The trek to Batad offers not only breathtaking views but also an immersive encounter with the local Ifugao way of life.

Trekking Adventures

Hiking Trails: Lace up your hiking boots for a trek through the terraced landscapes. Various trails cater to different fitness levels, offering opportunities to witness the terraces up close, interact with local communities, and enjoy panoramic vistas of the surrounding mountains.

Tappiya Falls: Reward your trek with a visit to Tappiya Falls in Batad. The waterfall, surrounded by lush greenery, provides a refreshing respite. Take a dip in the cool mountain waters and soak in the natural beauty that complements the cultural heritage of the region.

Practical Tips

Best Time to Visit: Plan your visit during the planting or harvesting seasons for a vivid display of the terraces. The months of April and May are particularly scenic when the rice paddies are lush green, while harvest time in September showcases golden landscapes.

Local Guides: Engage local guides to enhance your experience. Their knowledge of the terrain, cultural insights, and stories of the terraces add depth to your exploration.

Preserving a Cultural Treasure

UNESCO World Heritage Site: Recognized as a UNESCO World Heritage Site, the Banaue Rice Terraces face challenges from modernization and environmental factors. Support local conservation efforts by respecting the land, adhering to responsible tourism practices, and contributing to the local economy.

Visayas

Cebu City and Surroundings

Queen City of the South

Cebu City: Discover the vibrant heart of the Visayas region in Cebu City, often hailed as the "Queen City of the South." Explore the historical richness of Colon Street, the oldest street in the Philippines, and visit the Basilica del Santo Niño, home to the oldest Christian icon in the country.

Cultural Gems

Magellan's Cross: Witness the symbolic Magellan's Cross, planted by Portuguese explorer Ferdinand Magellan upon arriving in Cebu in 1521. The cross represents the birth of Christianity in the Philippines and stands within a chapel near the Basilica del Santo Niño.

Taoist Temple: Experience cultural diversity at the Taoist Temple, a serene haven that offers panoramic views of Cebu City. Immerse yourself in the teachings of Taoism and climb the steps to gain insights into the Chinese-Filipino heritage.

Island Adventures

Mactan Island: Escape to Mactan Island, just a bridge away from Cebu City. Lounge on pristine beaches, explore marine sanctuaries through island-hopping tours, and visit Lapu-Lapu Shrine commemorating the Battle of Mactan.

Oslob: Embark on a unique adventure in Oslob, where you can swim with whale sharks. This eco-friendly encounter provides a close-up experience with these gentle giants in their natural habitat.

Boracay Island

Tropical Paradise

White Beach: Sink your toes into the powdery white sands of White Beach, a 4-kilometer stretch that defines Boracay's tropical allure. Indulge in beachfront activities, from water sports to sunset strolls, and experience the vibrant nightlife along the beachfront.

Water Adventures

Water Sports: Dive into the crystal-clear waters surrounding Boracay and partake in an array of water sports. From parasailing and paddleboarding to snorkeling and scuba diving, the island caters to both thrill-seekers and those seeking a serene aquatic experience.

Puka Shell Beach: Escape the bustling White Beach and head to Puka Shell Beach, known for its coarser sand and serene atmosphere. Unwind in this quieter setting, collect unique shell souvenirs, and enjoy the natural beauty away from the crowds.

Vibrant Nightlife

D'Mall: Experience the lively atmosphere of D'Mall, a central hub offering shopping, dining, and entertainment options. Sample local and international cuisines, shop for souvenirs, and immerse yourself in the island's vibrant social scene.

Beach Parties: Boracay's nightlife comes alive with beach parties and fire dance performances. Join the festivities along the beach, where bars and clubs offer a mix of music, cocktails, and a lively ambiance.

Mindanao

Davao City and Davao Gulf

Diverse Metropolis

Davao City: Immerse yourself in the vibrant culture and natural beauty of Davao City, the largest city in Mindanao. Explore the bustling markets of Bankerohan, savor exotic fruits, and witness the iconic Philippine eagle at the Philippine Eagle Center.

Mount Apo

Trekking Adventure: Conquer the highest peak in the Philippines, Mount Apo. This towering volcano offers trekking enthusiasts a challenging yet rewarding journey with breathtaking views, diverse ecosystems, and a sense of accomplishment at its summit.

Hot Springs of Kapatagan: Unwind after your trek in the hot springs of Kapatagan, nestled at the foot of Mount Apo. Relax in the therapeutic waters surrounded by lush landscapes, providing a perfect post-trek rejuvenation.

Davao Gulf

Island-Hopping: Explore the islands and islets dotting Davao Gulf. Engage in island-hopping adventures, where you can discover pristine beaches, coral reefs, and marine sanctuaries. Talikud Island, with its white sands and vibrant underwater life, is a must-visit destination.

Samal Island: Just a short ferry ride from Davao City, Samal Island beckons with beautiful beaches and resorts. Enjoy water activities, visit the Monfort Bat Sanctuary, and relish the tranquil ambiance of this island retreat.

Siargao: Surfer's Paradise

Surfing Haven

Cloud 9: Embark on a surfing adventure at Cloud 9, Siargao's most famous surf spot. Known for its powerful waves and thrilling barrels, Cloud 9 attracts surfers from around the world. Beginners can also find surf schools along the coast for lessons.

Natural Wonders

Sugba Lagoon: Discover the enchanting Sugba Lagoon, surrounded by mangroves and limestone cliffs. Take a boat ride through crystal-clear waters, go paddleboarding, and marvel at the breathtaking scenery that defines this natural wonder.

Magpupungko Rock Pools: Visit the captivating rock pools of Magpupungko during low tide. Dive into the natural pools, formed by tidal movements, and enjoy the stunning ocean views against the backdrop of unique rock formations.

Island Vibes

General Luna: Immerse yourself in the island vibes of General Luna. Stroll along the vibrant boardwalk, indulge in fresh seafood at local eateries, and experience the laid-back atmosphere that characterizes this surfer's haven.

Island-Hopping: Explore the surrounding islands of Siargao. Del Carmen's Sohoton Cove National Park offers mystical lagoons, while Naked Island captivates with its pristine sands and clear waters.

Chapter Five: Top Attractions

Palawan

Puerto Princesa Underground River

Natural Wonder

World Heritage Site: Explore the mesmerizing Puerto Princesa Underground River, a UNESCO

World Heritage Site and one of the New Seven Wonders of Nature. Cruise along the subterranean river, marveling at limestone formations, stalactites, and stalagmites that create a captivating underground landscape.

Biodiversity

Flora and Fauna: Delve into the rich biodiversity of the underground river. Encounter unique species of bats, swiftlets, and diverse marine life within this ecological haven. The river's pristine ecosystem makes it a haven for nature enthusiasts and wildlife photographers.

Practical Tips

Permit and Tour: Secure the necessary permits to visit the underground river and opt for a guided boat tour. Knowledgeable guides provide insights into the geological formations and wildlife, enhancing your immersive experience.

Environmental Conservation: Contribute to the preservation of this natural wonder by adhering to eco-friendly practices. Follow designated paths, avoid touching formations, and participate in efforts to maintain the integrity of the underground river's ecosystem.

El Nido's Stunning Islands

Archipelago Paradise

Bacuit Bay: Embark on a journey to El Nido, nestled in Bacuit Bay, a haven of limestone karst cliffs, turquoise waters, and hidden lagoons. The archipelago's enchanting landscapes have earned El Nido its reputation as a tropical paradise.

Island-Hopping Adventures

Hidden Beach: Discover Hidden Beach, a secluded cove surrounded by towering cliffs. Accessible by boat, the beach provides a tranquil escape for swimming, snorkeling, and unwinding amidst the breathtaking scenery.

Big and Small Lagoons: Navigate the Big and Small Lagoons, renowned for their crystal-clear waters and dramatic limestone formations. Kayak through these natural wonders, immersing yourself in the serenity and beauty that define El Nido.

SUNSET AT CORONG-CORONG

Corong-Corong: Conclude your day with a mesmerizing sunset at Corong-Corong. This peaceful beach offers panoramic views of the sun setting over the Bacuit Archipelago, creating a picturesque backdrop for a serene evening.

Diverse Marine Life: El Nido's marine biodiversity is a treasure trove for snorkelers and divers. Explore vibrant coral reefs teeming with colorful fish, sea turtles, and other marine creatures, adding an aquatic dimension to your El Nido adventure.

Bohol

Chocolate Hills

Geological Marvel

Unique Landscape: Marvel at the extraordinary Chocolate Hills, a geological marvel that defines the landscape of Bohol. These conical limestone hills, numbering over a thousand, turn chocolate brown during the dry season, creating a surreal and enchanting panorama.

Viewing Points

Carmen: Visit the town of Carmen, where you'll find prime viewing points for the Chocolate Hills. The Chocolate Hills Complex offers an elevated platform, providing panoramic views of these natural wonders and the surrounding lush countryside.

Adventure Activities

ATV Adventures: Spice up your Chocolate Hills experience with ATV (All-Terrain Vehicle) adventures. Explore winding trails that lead to the hills, offering an exhilarating journey and a closer look at this unique landscape.

Chocolate Hills Adventure Park: For thrill-seekers, the Chocolate Hills Adventure Park offers adrenaline-pumping activities, including ziplining and bike zip adventures. Enjoy breathtaking views while engaging in exciting outdoor pursuits.

TARSIER CONSERVATION AREA

Tarsier Sanctuary

Tarsier Encounter: Visit the Tarsier Conservation Area to witness the world's smallest primates, the tarsiers. These tiny, wide-eyed creatures are endemic to the Philippines, and Bohol provides a sanctuary where visitors can observe them in their natural habitat.

Responsible Tourism

Guided Tours: Explore the Tarsier Conservation Area with guided tours that emphasize responsible and sustainable tourism. Knowledgeable guides provide information about the tarsiers' behavior, habitat, and the conservation efforts in place to protect these endangered species.

Habitat Preservation

Bohol Forest Reserve: The Tarsier Conservation Area often overlaps with the lush Bohol Forest Reserve. Immerse yourself in the beauty of this dense mahogany forest, where the conservation efforts not only benefit tarsiers but contribute to overall biodiversity and ecological balance.

Nocturnal Tarsier Watching: For a unique experience, consider joining a nocturnal tarsier watching tour. Witness these nocturnal primates in action as they hunt for insects under the cover of darkness, providing a different perspective on their behavior.

Chapter Six: Activities and Adventures

Scuba Diving in Tubbataha Reefs Natural Park

Underwater Paradise

Tubbataha Reefs Natural Park: Dive into the mesmerizing world beneath the surface at Tubbataha Reefs Natural Park. Recognized as a UNESCO World Heritage Site and located in the Sulu Sea, this marine sanctuary is a haven for scuba diving enthusiasts seeking unparalleled underwater beauty.

Dive Highlights

Coral Gardens: Explore vibrant coral gardens teeming with a kaleidoscope of marine life. Tubbataha is home to a stunning array of coral species, providing a backdrop for encounters with tropical fish, turtles, and other captivating creatures.

Shark Encounters: Witness the grace of sharks as they glide through the crystal-clear waters.

Tubbataha is known for shark sightings, including reef sharks and hammerhead sharks, creating thrilling moments for experienced divers.

Dive Sites

Delsan Wreck: Discover the Delsan Wreck, a sunken cargo ship that has become an artificial reef. This site attracts diverse marine species, making it an exciting exploration for underwater photographers and marine enthusiasts.

Amos Rock: Experience the vibrant marine ecosystem around Amos Rock. From schools of fish to majestic pelagics, this site offers a dynamic underwater landscape for divers of varying skill levels.

Practical Tips

Diving Seasons: Plan your dive during the Tubbataha diving season, typically from March to June when weather conditions are optimal. During this period, the park is open to liveaboard dive trips, providing an immersive and extended diving experience.

Liveaboard Excursions: Consider joining a liveaboard diving expedition to fully appreciate the remote and pristine nature of Tubbataha. Liveaboards offer multiple dives per day, allowing you to explore the diverse dive sites and marine ecosystems of the park.

Conservation and Responsible Diving

Preserving Marine Life: Tubbataha Reefs Natural Park emphasizes marine conservation, and divers are encouraged to practice responsible diving.

Follow guidelines, avoid touching marine life or coral, and contribute to the park's conservation efforts to ensure its continued natural beauty.

Permit Requirements: Obtain the necessary permits before embarking on your Tubbataha diving adventure. Check with local authorities or dive operators for up-to-date information on permits, park regulations, and dive logistics.

Hiking in Mount Pulag

Majestic Summit

Mount Pulag: Embark on a hiking adventure to the summit of Mount Pulag, one of the highest peaks in the Philippines. This majestic mountain, located in the Cordillera Range, offers breathtaking views of sea clouds, creating a surreal and awe-inspiring landscape.

Hiking Trails

Ambangeg Trail: Choose the Ambangeg Trail for a relatively easier ascent to the summit. This trail provides stunning views of the grassland slopes and the iconic sea of clouds, making it a popular choice for both beginners and experienced hikers.

Akiki Trail: For a more challenging and scenic route, consider the Akiki Trail. This trail takes you through mossy forests, steep slopes, and diverse ecosystems, culminating in a rewarding panoramic view from the summit.

Camping Experience

Camping at the Summit: Extend your Mount Pulag adventure by camping at the summit. Witness the sunrise, as the sea of clouds below transforms into a mesmerizing display of colors. Camping permits are required, so plan and secure your arrangements in advance.

Stargazing: Enjoy a spectacular night sky at the summit, where minimal light pollution allows for an unparalleled stargazing experience. The cool mountain air and clear skies create an ideal setting for astronomy enthusiasts.

Practical Tips

Permit and Registration: Obtain the necessary permits and register with the local authorities before your hike. Mount Pulag is a protected area, and responsible tourism practices are crucial to preserve its natural beauty.

Proper Gear: Equip yourself with proper hiking gear, including sturdy footwear, layered clothing, and essential camping equipment. The weather at Mount Pulag can be unpredictable, so be prepared for both warmth and cold.

Island Hopping in Coron

Coron's Archipelago

Coron: Embark on an island-hopping adventure in the stunning archipelago of Coron. This Palawan gem is renowned for its crystal-clear waters, limestone cliffs, and a myriad of picturesque islands and lagoons.

Must-Visit Islands and Lagoons

Kayangan Lake: Explore the iconic Kayangan Lake, often touted as the cleanest lake in the Philippines. Hike up to the viewpoint for a panoramic sight of the lake surrounded by towering limestone cliffs.

Twin Lagoon: Experience the unique beauty of Twin Lagoon, where warm and cool waters meet. Navigate through a small crevice or swim between the lagoons during low tide for a captivating natural encounter.

Coral Gardens and Shipwrecks

Snorkeling and Diving: Dive into vibrant coral gardens and explore Japanese shipwrecks from World War II submerged in Coron's waters. The marine life and underwater landscapes make Coron a haven for snorkelers and divers.

Malcapuya Island: Unwind on the white sandy beaches of Malcapuya Island. With its pristine shores and turquoise waters, it offers a serene escape and is often less crowded than other tourist spots.

Practical Tips

Island-Hopping Tours: Join island-hopping tours offered by local operators to make the most of your Coron adventure. These tours usually cover multiple attractions in a day, providing a comprehensive exploration of the archipelago.

Responsible Tourism: Practice responsible tourism by respecting the marine environment. Follow guidelines for snorkeling and diving, avoid stepping on coral reefs, and contribute to the preservation of Coron's natural beauty.

Chapter Seven: Culinary Delights

Filipino Cuisine Overview

Flavorful Fusion

Culinary Diversity: Filipino cuisine is a delightful fusion of indigenous, Spanish, Chinese, and American influences, resulting in a diverse and flavorful culinary landscape. Each region boasts its unique dishes, creating a rich tapestry of tastes and textures.

Signature Dishes

Adobo: Considered the unofficial national dish, Adobo features meat (usually pork or chicken) marinated in soy sauce, vinegar, garlic, and spices, then simmered until tender. The result is a savory and slightly tangy masterpiece.

Sinigang: A comforting and sour tamarind-based soup, Sinigang incorporates various meats (pork, beef, shrimp) and an array of vegetables. The sourness, balanced with savory flavors, makes it a beloved Filipino comfort food.

Lechon: Celebrations are incomplete without Lechon, a festive dish of roasted whole pig. The crispy skin and succulent meat create a gastronomic experience that's a must-try during special occasions.

Kare-Kare: This oxtail stew in peanut sauce is a savory delight. Paired with bagoong (fermented shrimp paste), it offers a unique blend of flavors and textures.

Street Food Extravaganza

Balut: Adventurous eaters can try Balut, a fertilized duck embryo boiled and typically enjoyed with a dash of salt and sometimes vinegar. It's a popular street food known for its distinct taste and texture.

Isaw: Grilled chicken or pork intestines on skewers, Isaw is a flavorful and affordable street snack often enjoyed with a vinegar-based dipping sauce.

Fish Balls: Fish Balls, deep-fried fish or fish-based balls served with a variety of sauces, are a ubiquitous and tasty street food found throughout the Philippines.

Sweet Indulgences

Halo-Halo: Beat the heat with Halo-Halo, a refreshing dessert that combines shaved ice with a medley of ingredients like sweet beans, jellies, fruits, and leche flan, topped with evaporated milk.

Leche Flan: This caramel custard, reminiscent of Spanish flan, is a velvety and sweet delight often enjoyed during celebrations.

Regional Specialties

Bicol Express: Hailing from the Bicol region, Bicol Express is a spicy pork dish cooked with coconut milk, shrimp paste, and plenty of chili peppers, delivering a kick of flavor.

Laing: Another Bicolano gem, Laing features dried taro leaves cooked in coconut milk with chili peppers, creating a rich and spicy dish.

Must Try Dishes

Sinigang

Tangy Comfort: Sinigang is a comforting tamarind-based soup that embodies the Filipino palate. The sour broth, complemented by various meats (pork, beef, shrimp) and an assortment of vegetables, creates a flavorful and heartwarming dish.

Lechon Kawali

Crispy Delight: Indulge in the crispy goodness of Lechon Kawali, deep-fried pork belly. The result is a crackling exterior and tender meat, often served with liver sauce or vinegar for an extra kick.

Chicken Adobo

National Favorite: Chicken Adobo, a staple in Filipino households, features chicken simmered in soy sauce, vinegar, garlic, and spices. The slow-cooking process infuses the meat with a savory and slightly tangy flavor.

Kare-Kare

Peanut Perfection: Kare-Kare is a delectable oxtail stew with a rich peanut sauce. Often accompanied by bagoong (fermented shrimp paste), it offers a delightful combination of savory and nutty flavors.

Halo-Halo

Cooling Creation: Beat the tropical heat with Halo-Halo, a shaved ice dessert that combines a variety of ingredients like sweet beans, jellies, fruits, and leche flan. Topped with evaporated milk, it's a refreshing and colorful treat.

Street Food Adventures

Isaw

Grilled Delight: Isaw, skewered and grilled chicken or pork intestines, is a popular street food known for its smoky flavor. Enjoy it with a side of vinegar-based dipping sauce.

Fish Balls

Street Snacking: Fish Balls, deep-fried fish or fish-based balls, are a ubiquitous street food found on corners and bustling markets. Dip them in a variety of sauces for an affordable and tasty snack.

Balut

Adventurous Bite: For the daring, try Balut—a boiled fertilized duck egg. Sprinkle a bit of salt and, for some, a dash of vinegar, to experience the unique textures and flavors of this Filipino street food delicacy.

Taho

Sweet Morning Treat: Taho is a sweet morning treat consisting of warm silken tofu topped with arnibal (caramelized sugar) and sago pearls (similar to tapioca). It's often peddled by Taho vendors calling out their distinctive "Taho" chants.

Turon

Sweet Banana Rolls: Satisfy your sweet tooth with Turon, banana slices and sometimes jackfruit rolled in a spring roll wrapper, then fried until crispy. The result is a delightful combination of sweet and crunchy flavors.

Chapter Eight: Cultural Experiences
Festivals and Celebrations

Sinulog Festival

Cebu City: Immerse yourself in the vibrant Sinulog Festival, held in Cebu City every January. This grand celebration honors the Sto. Niño, the Holy Child, with a lively parade featuring street dancing, colorful costumes, and religious processions. Join the festivities that blend religious traditions with energetic performances.

Ati-Atihan Festival

Kalibo, Aklan: Head to Kalibo, Aklan, for the lively Ati-Atihan Festival, often hailed as the "Mother of All Philippine Festivals." This week-long celebration, held in January, involves tribal dance competitions, street parties, and a vibrant parade where participants paint their bodies in black and don vibrant costumes.

Panagbenga Festival

Baguio City: Experience the Panagbenga Festival, also known as the Flower Festival, in Baguio City every February. This month-long celebration showcases vibrant floral floats, street dancing, and cultural events. The Grand Float Parade is a highlight, featuring creatively decorated floats adorned with fresh flowers.

Pahiyas Festival

Lucban, Quezon: Visit Lucban, Quezon, during the Pahiyas Festival in May. This colorful harvest festival transforms the town into a visual feast with houses adorned in colorful kipings (decorative rice wafers), fruits, and vegetables. Celebrate the bounties of nature with lively street decorations and a gastronomic journey through local delicacies.

Dinagyang Festival

Iloilo City: Join the energetic Dinagyang Festival in Iloilo City every January. This religious and cultural celebration pays homage to the Sto. Niño and features street dancing competitions, drumbeats, and a vibrant atmosphere. The Ati Tribe competition showcases performers in elaborate costumes portraying historical and cultural themes.

Moriones Festival

Marinduque: Witness the unique Moriones Festival in Marinduque during Holy Week. This religious event involves locals donning colorful masks and costumes depicting Roman soldiers (Moriones). The festival reenacts the story of Longinus, a Roman centurion converted to Christianity, and adds a theatrical touch to Holy Week observances.

Kadayawan Festival

Davao City: Experience the Kadayawan Festival in Davao City every August. Celebrating the city's cultural heritage and bountiful harvest, the festival features street parades, floral floats, and cultural performances. Indulge in the week-long festivities that showcase the rich diversity of indigenous cultures in the region.

MassKara Festival

Bacolod City: Dive into the lively MassKara Festival in Bacolod City every October. Known for its vibrant masks, street dancing, and electric atmosphere, the festival is a symbol of Bacolod's resilience and festive spirit. Enjoy the dazzling street performances and join in the revelry during this "City of Smiles" celebration.

Traditional Arts and Crafts

Weaving in Ifugao

Banaue, Ifugao: Explore the traditional art of weaving in Banaue, Ifugao. Witness skilled artisans create intricate patterns and designs on looms, producing the vibrant and symbolic fabrics used in traditional Ifugao attire. Purchase handwoven products like blankets and clothing as souvenirs, supporting the rich heritage of Ifugao craftsmanship.

Pottery in Sagada

Sagada, Mountain Province: Discover the ancient art of pottery in Sagada. Local artisans shape clay into various forms using traditional methods, producing functional and decorative pottery. Participate in pottery workshops to learn the techniques and create your unique masterpiece, providing a hands-on experience with Sagada's artistic heritage.

T'nalak Weaving in South Cotabato

Lake Sebu, South Cotabato: Immerse yourself in T'nalak weaving, an indigenous craft of the T'boli people in Lake Sebu. The intricate process involves hand-weaving abaca fibers into vibrant patterns, with each design holding cultural significance. Witness the craftsmanship, and perhaps acquire a T'nalak piece as a meaningful memento.

Shellcraft in Cebu

Mactan Island, Cebu: Explore the art of shellcraft on Mactan Island. Skilled artisans create intricate designs using shells, turning them into jewelry, decor, and functional items. Visit local workshops to see the delicate process and purchase unique shellcraft pieces that reflect the island's coastal beauty.

Historical Sites and Museums

Intramuros in Manila

Manila: Step into the historical heart of Manila by visiting Intramuros. This walled city, built during Spanish colonial rule, features well-preserved structures like Fort Santiago and San Agustin Church. Explore cobbled streets, museums, and landmarks that offer a glimpse into the Philippines' colonial past.

Banaue Rice Terraces

Banaue, Ifugao: Marvel at the Banaue Rice Terraces, often referred to as the "Eighth Wonder of the World." Carved into the mountains over 2,000 years ago by Ifugao ancestors, these terraces showcase ingenious agricultural engineering. Visit the Banaue Museum to delve into the cultural and historical significance of these stunning landscapes.

National Museum of the Philippines

Manila: Delve into Filipino art, history, and culture at the National Museum of the Philippines. Explore the National Museum Complex, which includes the National Museum of Fine Arts, National Museum of Anthropology, and National Museum of Natural History. Admire priceless artworks, artifacts, and exhibits that narrate the nation's story.

Corregidor Island

Cavite: Take a journey to Corregidor Island, a historical site known for its role during World War II. Explore the ruins, tunnels, and memorials that bear witness to the island's wartime history. Visit the Malinta Tunnel, Pacific War Memorial, and Battery Way to gain insights into the events that shaped the Philippines during the war.

Chapter Nine: Practical Tips

Transportation within the Philippines

Domestic Flights

Hub Airports: Utilize major airports such as Ninoy Aquino International Airport (MNL) in Manila, Mactan-Cebu International Airport (CEB) in Cebu, and Clark International Airport (CRK) in Pampanga for domestic flights. Airlines like Philippine Airlines, Cebu Pacific, and

AirAsia connect major cities and tourist destinations.

Booking in Advance: Secure domestic flight tickets in advance, especially during peak travel seasons, to ensure availability and potentially benefit from lower fares.

Buses and Vans

Inter-Island Travel: Buses and vans are common modes of transportation for inter-island travel. Major bus companies operate comfortable long-distance buses, while vans provide more flexibility for shorter routes.

Public Terminals: Buses and vans usually depart from public terminals. Be sure to check schedules and arrive early to secure your seat, especially during busy travel periods.

Jeepneys and Tricycles

Local Transport: Jeepneys and tricycles are popular modes of local transportation, especially in cities and towns. Jeepneys are shared open-air vehicles, and tricycles are three-wheeled motorcycles with sidecars.

Negotiate Fares: When using tricycles, negotiate fares beforehand, as they might not have meters. Jeepney fares are often fixed and displayed inside the vehicle.

Ferries and Boats

Island-Hopping: Ferries and boats are essential for island-hopping adventures. Major ferry terminals are found in ports like Batangas, Cebu, and Dumaguete.

Weather Considerations: Be mindful of weather conditions, especially during the typhoon season, as ferry schedules may be affected.

Renting Vehicles

Car Rentals: Renting a car can provide flexibility, especially when exploring less accessible areas. International and local car rental companies operate in major cities and airports.

Driving Considerations: Familiarize yourself with local traffic rules and driving conditions. Keep in mind that traffic in major cities can be congested, and road conditions may vary.

Transportation Apps

Ride-Hailing Services: Utilize ride-hailing services like Grab for convenient and reliable transportation in urban areas. These services often provide fare estimates and enhance safety during travels.

Navigation Apps: Use navigation apps like Google Maps for real-time directions, estimated travel times, and alternative routes, especially when exploring unfamiliar areas.

Traveling Off-Peak

Avoiding Peak Hours: Plan your travels during off-peak hours to avoid heavy traffic, especially in metropolitan areas. This can contribute to a smoother and more enjoyable journey.

Flexibility: Be flexible with your travel plans, as unexpected delays or changes in schedules may occur, especially in regions prone to weather-related disruptions.

Accommodations

DIVERSE OPTIONS

Variety of Choices: Choose accommodations based on your preferences and budget. Options range from luxury hotels and resorts to budget-friendly hostels, guesthouses, and local inns.

Booking Platforms: Utilize online booking platforms such as Booking.com, Agoda, or Airbnb to explore a wide range of accommodations, read reviews, and secure the best deals.

Communication and Connectivity

SIM Cards

Local SIM Cards: Purchase a local SIM card upon arrival for better communication and mobile data services. Major carriers include Globe Telecom, Smart Communications, and DITO Telecommunity.

Data Plans: Consider data plans that suit your needs, especially if you plan to navigate using maps, stay connected with family, or share your travel experiences on social media.

Wi-Fi Availability

Hotels and Cafes: Most hotels, cafes, and public spaces offer Wi-Fi. Confirm Wi-Fi availability with your accommodation and explore nearby cafes for reliable internet access.

Connectivity in Remote Areas: In more remote areas, be prepared for limited connectivity. Download offline maps and important information in advance.

Packing Tips

Weather-Appropriate Clothing

Diverse Climate: Pack clothing suitable for the diverse climate. Light and breathable fabrics are ideal for tropical weather, while a light jacket or sweater may be necessary for cooler evenings or highland destinations.

Rainy Season Considerations: If traveling during the rainy season, include a waterproof jacket, umbrella, and quick-drying clothing in your packing list.

Travel Adapters

Power Outlets: Bring a universal travel adapter to ensure your electronic devices can be charged. The Philippines generally uses Type A, B, and C sockets with a standard voltage of 220V and a frequency of 60Hz.

Essentials

Medications and First Aid Kit: Include any necessary medications and a basic first aid kit in your luggage. While pharmacies are available, it's advisable to have essential items on hand.

Travel Documents: Keep your travel documents, including passport, visa, and any required permits, in a secure and easily accessible location.

Daypack

Exploration Gear: Pack a daypack for excursions, hikes, or island hopping. Include essentials like water, sunscreen, a hat, insect repellent, and a small towel.

Reusable Water Bottle: Stay hydrated by carrying a reusable water bottle. Some areas may not have easily accessible drinking water, so having your bottle is convenient and eco-friendly.

Money Matters

Local Currency: Carry sufficient local currency, especially when traveling to remote areas where card payments may not be widely accepted.

ATM Access: Use ATMs in major cities for cash withdrawals. Inform your bank of your travel dates to avoid any issues with international transactions.

Light Snacks

Travel-Friendly Snacks: Pack some light snacks for the journey, especially if you have dietary preferences or are traveling to areas with limited food options.

Reusable Utensils: Consider carrying reusable utensils to reduce single-use plastic waste when enjoying local street food.

CHAPTER TEN: SUSTAINABILITY AND RESPONSIBLE TRAVEL
Ecotourism Initiatives

Tubbataha Reefs Natural Park

Marine Conservation: Support the conservation efforts at Tubbataha Reefs Natural Park, a UNESCO World Heritage Site. Choose dive operators and liveaboard trips that prioritize sustainable practices, contribute to marine conservation, and adhere to park regulations.

Eco-friendly Diving: Opt for eco-friendly diving practices, such as reef-friendly sunscreen, responsible diving behavior, and participation in organized reef clean-up activities to minimize the ecological impact.

Masungi Georeserve

Conservation and Education: Explore Masungi Georeserve, a geopark in Rizal province dedicated to conservation and environmental education. Choose guided tours that promote responsible exploration, respect for nature, and contribute to the georeserve's conservation projects.

Trail Preservation: Follow designated trails and guidelines during your visit to minimize environmental impact. Masungi Georeserve emphasizes sustainable tourism practices to protect its unique limestone formations and biodiversity.

Apo Reef Natural Park

Reef Conservation: Contribute to reef conservation at Apo Reef Natural Park in Occidental Mindoro. Select dive operators and boat services that adhere to responsible tourism guidelines, including waste management and protection of marine ecosystems.

Educational Tours: Participate in educational tours that highlight the importance of marine conservation and responsible diving. Support initiatives that aim to preserve the rich biodiversity of Apo Reef.

Mayon Skyline View Deck

Community Involvement: Visit the Mayon Skyline View Deck in Albay and choose tours that engage with local communities. Support initiatives that involve indigenous communities, promote cultural exchange, and contribute to community development.

Responsible Photography: Practice responsible photography by respecting local customs and seeking permission before taking pictures, particularly if capturing images of individuals or community spaces.

BANAUE RICE TERRACES

Cultural Preservation: When exploring the Banaue Rice Terraces, a UNESCO World Heritage Site, choose guided tours that emphasize cultural preservation. Learn about the traditional farming methods and the importance of preserving this ancient cultural landscape.

Local Crafts and Souvenirs: Support local artisans and communities by purchasing handmade crafts and souvenirs. This contributes to the economic sustainability of the region.

Responsible Island Hopping in Palawan

Environmental Practices: Engage in responsible island hopping in Palawan by choosing operators committed to environmental protection. Ensure that boat tours adhere to waste management practices and educate visitors on the importance of preserving the pristine island ecosystems.

Leave No Trace: Follow the principles of "Leave No Trace" by respecting the natural environment, disposing of waste properly, and avoiding damage to coral reefs and marine life during snorkeling or diving activities.

Environmental Awareness in Sagada

Respect Local Traditions: In Sagada, participate in eco-friendly activities that promote environmental awareness. Respect local traditions, including the practice of burying the deceased in hanging coffins, by engaging with cultural sites in a responsible manner.

Leave No Trace Hiking: When hiking in Sagada, follow Leave No Trace principles, stay on designated trails, and avoid disturbing natural habitats. Support community initiatives that aim to balance tourism with environmental conservation.

Responsible Diving and Snorkeling Practices

Coral Conservation

Mindful Diving: Practice mindful diving by avoiding contact with coral reefs. Maintain buoyancy control and be cautious with equipment to prevent unintentional damage to delicate marine ecosystems.

No Touching Policy: Adhere to a "no touching" policy for marine life. Resist the temptation to handle or disturb underwater creatures, as this helps protect their natural behaviors and habitats.

Sustainable Diving Operators

Research Dive Centers: Choose dive operators with a commitment to sustainable and responsible practices. Look for certifications such as the Green Fins certification, which indicates a dedication to environmentally friendly diving operations.

Eco-friendly Products: Use reef-safe sunscreen and environmentally friendly dive gear to minimize the impact on marine life and coral reefs. Opt for gear that avoids harmful chemicals and materials.

Marine Life Etiquette

Maintain a Safe Distance: Observe marine life from a safe and respectful distance. Avoid chasing or disturbing animals, and allow them to carry on with their natural behaviors without interference.

Buoyancy Control: Enhance your buoyancy control skills to avoid accidental contact with the seafloor or coral. Attend buoyancy clinics or workshops to improve your diving skills.

Supporting Local Communities

Local Businesses

Eat Local: Support local restaurants and eateries to experience authentic flavors and contribute directly to the local economy. Choose establishments that emphasize the use of locally sourced ingredients.

Shop Locally: Purchase souvenirs and goods from local markets and artisans. This ensures that your spending directly benefits the community and promotes the preservation of traditional crafts.

Cultural Respect

Respect Local Customs: Familiarize yourself with and respect local customs and traditions. This includes appropriate attire, greetings, and behavior when interacting with community members.

Learn Basic Phrases: Learn a few basic phrases in the local language to enhance communication and show respect for the local culture. Locals often appreciate visitors making an effort to connect in their native language.

Community-based Tourism

Homestays and Local Accommodations: Consider staying in homestays or locally owned accommodations to directly support community-based tourism initiatives. This provides a more immersive experience and channels funds back into the community.

Participate in Community Activities: Engage in community activities or cultural experiences offered by local organizations. This fosters a deeper understanding of the community's way of life and contributes to sustainable tourism.

Volunteer Opportunities

Community Volunteering: Explore volunteer opportunities that align with community needs. This could involve participating in local environmental initiatives, educational programs, or community development projects.

Responsible Wildlife Interactions: If participating in wildlife-related activities, choose those that prioritize animal welfare and conservation. Avoid supporting activities that exploit or harm animals for entertainment purposes.

Conclusion
Final Thoughts

Embarking on a journey through the Philippines is not just about exploring its breathtaking landscapes, vibrant cultures, and diverse ecosystems—it's an opportunity to embrace responsible travel. From the bustling streets of Manila to the serene beauty of Palawan's islands, every step unveils a tapestry of experiences and a chance to make a positive impact.

Remember, responsible travel is more than just leaving footprints; it's about leaving a positive mark on the places you visit. Support local communities, engage in sustainable practices, and cherish the natural wonders that make the Philippines a truly remarkable destination.

Memories to Take Home

As you conclude your Philippine adventure, take home more than just photographs. Capture the warmth of Filipino hospitality, the flavors of diverse cuisines, and the echoes of laughter from vibrant festivals. The memories you've created, the connections you've forged, and the cultural insights gained are the true souvenirs of your journey.

In case of emergencies in the Philippines, here are some important contact numbers:

- ✓ Emergency Hotline: 911
- ✓ Philippine National Police (PNP): 117 or (02) 723-0401

- ✓ Philippine Red Cross: (02) 8790-2300
- ✓ Bureau of Fire Protection (BFP): 117 or (02) 426-0219
- ✓ Medical Emergency (National Poison Control Center): (02) 8-711-6828

Printed in Great Britain
by Amazon